This book is dedicated
to all children and all
the special people
who help them

Nearly 25 million people from all around the world, challenged by various disabilities, are discovering the limitlessness of their creative potential through VSA programs and activities.

Very Special Arts was founded on the national level in 1974 as an educational affiliate of the John F. Kennedy Center for the Performing Arts, and has been established as a non-profit organization in Michigan since 1978. VSA/Michigan-Grand Rapids has been opening creative doors for the special needs community of Kent County since 1985, when it became a community project of the Junior League of Grand Rapids, Michigan, Inc.

A special thank you to the following,
whose support has made this book a reality:

The Grand Rapids Foundation
South Kent AMBUCS
Sandra DeGroot
City Media
Dennis Grantz
Jody Rosasco Grantz
Grand Rapids Kiwanis Foundation
The Junior League of Grand Rapids, MI, Inc.

© 1992 Very Special Arts/Michigan-Grand Rapids
A project of the Junior League of Grand Rapids, Michigan, Inc.

Printed and bound by Impresora Donneco Internacional, S.A. de C.V.,
a subsidiary of R.R. Donnelley & Sons Company.

Manufactured in Mexico

ISBN 0-9634 927-0-5

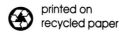 printed on recycled paper

SOMETHING SPECIAL

The Authors

Back Row: Kevin, Tjasse, Sarah, Chris A., Stephanie, Dustin
Front Row: Nick, Barton, Jonathan
Not Pictured: David
(Photo taken two years after writing)
Bottom Left: Greg

Some children need wheelchairs to help them move around and go places.

Some children need hearing aids to help them hear and talk better.

Some children
need braces
on their legs to
help them walk.

Some children
can't see and
need a cane
to help them
find their way.

But all children would like to paint and dance and sing and make things.

How will these children

ever be able to do all

these wonderful things

...like you do?

**VERY
SPECIAL
ARTS
MICHIGAN**

There is a special group
of people who want all children to
dance and sing and draw.

This group is called Very Special Arts.

They use artists from all over the city
to help special needs children.

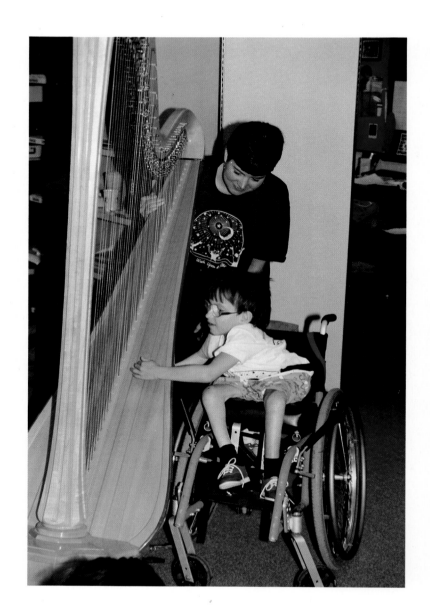

During the school year, an artist comes to the classroom and teaches the children.

One class learned to do origami, the art of paper folding from Japan.

Other children learned something about other countries
while they learned a special craft.

Another class went to a stained glass window store to make a kaleidoscope!

They said, "It was kind of hard to do. We used solder to put the glass together. We melted it with a soldering iron.

Vicky helped us and our teacher helped, too. It was lots of fun!"

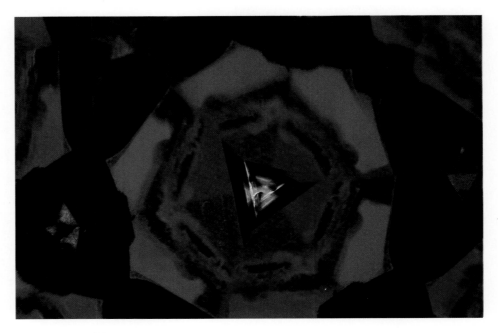

Children in our city
have learned to
do many things.

Here are
some pictures
of some very special
artists at work.

Learning to draw can be fun.

Artwork
by
Chris

Artwork by Andy

Artwork
by
Chris

Chris 12
ParkView

Elvin
Mayfield

Artwork
by
Elvin

Some of the children
who live in our city
have learned to
work with both
35 millimeter
and pinhole
cameras.

Here are
some of the pictures
they took.

Pinhole photo
by
Kowase

Pinhole photos
by
Amy

20

Every June, our city has a big art festival downtown, and thousands of people come to enjoy music, dance, art and good food.

Members of a physically impaired class in wheelchairs, gifted and talented students from our city and the Living Light Dance Co. (a group of developmentally disabled students), were the opening stage act of Festival.

In May, many artists and
children get together for a
huge Very Special Arts Festival.

Children get to explore
various areas of art
during mini-workshops.

Wheelchair Painting!

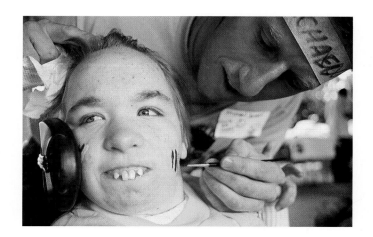

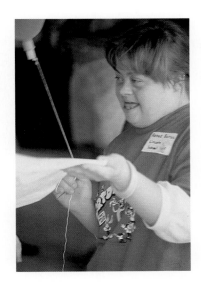

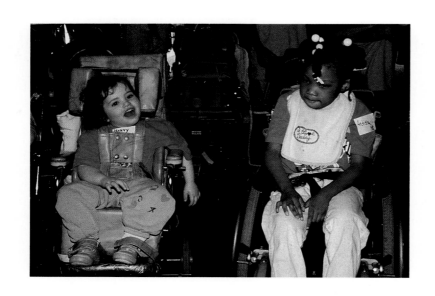

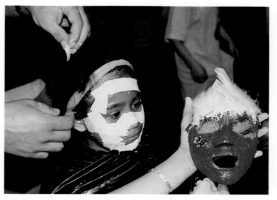

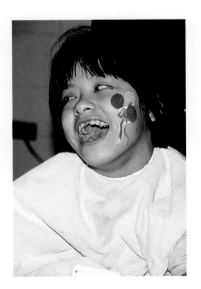

Throughout the day, special children celebrate the joys of creativity through Very Special Arts!

GLOSSARY

Special Education is a special way of teaching children with impairments. Because of their handicaps, these children can't always learn the same way other children can, in regular classes. But they can learn from teachers who have been trained to use special techniques of educating.

A **hearing impaired** person is someone whose hearing has been damaged through an illness or an accident; or never fully developed before birth. We say they have a hearing impairment because their sense of hearing doesn't work perfectly.

Hearing aids are devices that go in your ear to make the sound louder. They can help you hear better, but not perfectly.

Cochlear Implants are operations that restore some hearing in deaf people. One part of an electronic instrument is implanted in the temporal ear bone and the other part is worn as a pocket hearing aid. This medical procedure can effectively increase a person's potential for hearing.

TDD stands for Telecommunication Device for the Deaf. This is a machine that allows deaf people to use a telephone, by printing the message on a screen. Even though deaf people can't hear the message, they can see it.

A **visually impaired** person is someone whose <u>eyes</u> have been damaged through illness or accident, or never fully developed before birth.

Braille is a system of little raised bumps on paper made by a special machine so visually impaired people can read with their fingers. Recently, braille has also been added to some elevators, automatic banking machines, and even the menus in restaurants.

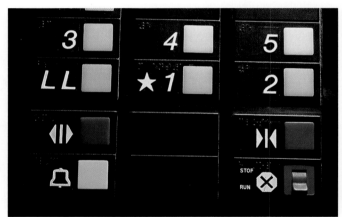

A **mentally impaired** person is someone whose <u>brain</u> has been damaged through an illness or accident, or never fully developed before birth.

A **physically impaired** person is someone whose <u>body</u> has been damaged through an illness or accident, or never fully developed before birth.

A **prosthetic device**, or **prosthesis**, is a tool, like a plastic hand or leg, that attaches to a person's body to help him or her move or walk.

Braces are pieces of metal or plastic that wrap around your body to give you strength when you stand up, sit or move.

A **wheelchair** is a special chair with wheels that enables a person who cannot walk to either move him or herself around or to be pushed around by someone else.

With a wheelchair, people who can't walk can go almost anywhere.

The End